IMAGES OF ENGLAND

Around Billingham

FREDERICK M. DAWSON OBE. Fred Dawson served from 1947 until 1967 as the Clerk to Billingham Urban District Council. With dynamic energy, efficiency and vision, and an enthusiastic Council, he transformed Billingham into a large and progressive town. So great was his impact that he was dubbed 'Mr Billingham' and the new town centre 'Dawson City'.

IMAGES OF ENGLAND

Around Billingham

Vera Chapman

NONSUCH

SYNTHONIA CLUB CRICKET FIELD. This view from Belasis Avenue illustrates the close association between leisure, Garden City-inspired housing and ICI. Chilton House (ICI Main Offices, built in 1927) on the left faced the UDC's Chilton Estate and ICI's Roscoe Road and Mill Lane houses. Chilton Lane led to ICI's West Gate entrance and Nitrates Avenue. (See page 110.)

First published 1996
This new pocket edition 2006
Images unchanged from first edition

Nonsuch Publishing Limited
The Mill, Brimscombe Port,
Stroud, Gloucestershire, GL5 2QG
www.nonsuch-publishing.com

Nonsuch Publishing is an imprint of Tempus Publishing Group

British Library Cataloguing in Publication Data.
A catalogue record for this book is available from the British Library.

ISBN 1-84588-251-2

Typesetting and origination by Nonsuch Publishing Limited
Printed in Great Britain by Oaklands Book Services Limited

Contents

Introduction 7

1. Billingham Village, Haverton Hill and Port Clarence 9

2. Billingham between the Wars 21

3. Around the New Town Centre 35

4. The Forum: Sport, Theatre and International Festival 53

5. Northward Expansion: Schools of the Sixties and Seventies 69

6. ICI – The Early Years:
Start-up, Products, Oil-from-Coal and Transport 87

7. ICI People at Work and at Leisure 109

Acknowledgements 128

CASTNER SODIUM PLANT, BILLINGHAM SOUTH SITE. Devised by H.Y. Castner in 1890, an improved process was used at ICI Billingham from 1930 until 1952. Protective clothing included boots or wooden-soled clogs.

Introduction

A Saxon settlement from around the seventh century, the 'home of Billa's people' nestles around a green beside the parish church of St Cuthbert. The church, remarkable for its Saxon nave and tower, is a landmark above the steep-sided valley of the Billingham Beck near its confluence with the River Tees in the south-east corner of historic County Durham.

Following the Conquest, William I gave lands here to his retainer, John of Belasis, and to the Prior of Durham monastery. Each built himself a moated manor house, named 'Belasis' (beautiful site) and 'Beaulieu' (beautiful place). In the seventeenth century the common fields of the peasants were enclosed, and farmsteads moved away from the village. By 1801 only 335 people were recorded as living here but the nineteenth century saw development to the east at Haverton Hill and Port Clarence, when the Clarence Railway and coal staithes, iron and salt and glass works, and some 4,500 people arrived. Billingham village itself, isolated by the marshes of Billingham Beck, the River Tees and its estuary, remained rural until the end of the First World War.

That war was to be a turning point, however. The loss through enemy action of ships and of Chilean nitrates for explosives led to the setting up of the Furness shipbuilding yard at Haverton Hill and a Ministry of Munitions factory to make synthetic nitrates next to Billingham village.

In 1919 the unfinished factory was taken over by Brunner Mond, and in 1920 the Synthetic Ammonia and Nitrates Company was formed to manufacture synthetic nitrates for fertilizers, a case of 'swords into ploughshares'. In 1926 the firm became a part of Imperial Chemical Industries Ltd (ICI), and in 1929 the Billingham site became ICI (Fertilizers and Synthetic Products) Ltd.

A vast anhydrite deposit deep beneath the factory was worked from 1923. A salt bed to the east allowed brine extraction for caustic soda and chlorine. The Government was concerned to offset dependence on imported oil, the world's known reserves of which were then thought to be finite. In the 1920s and '30s new technology was pioneered at Billingham to make oil and petrol from coal.

The Billingham site grew rapidly, with a complex of interlocking processes. Organization and products changed over the years, and the Second World War brought a temporary reversion to war-essential production. In 1958 the traditional ammonia-based chemistry was assigned to Billingham Division, while organic products, developed since the war, became Heavy Organic Chemicals Division (HOC). In the 1960s oil and natural gas displaced old technology, coal wagons and coke ovens went, and some products ceased.

Billingham Division, renamed Agricultural Division, later employed over 300 graduate scientists in fundamental and applied research. Having become a world-leading chemical producer, it also became the site landlord providing services for five ICI Divisions. At its height around 19,000 people were employed on the 1,000 acre site with its eighty miles of standard gauge rail track, twenty locomotives, around 1,000 railway wagons, and its own wharves along the River Tees.

Many chemical products are unfamiliar to the general public and do not reach them direct, being the ingredients or catalysts for further manufactures or specialist users. What was and is familiar is an exciting landscape of dramatic structures of gigantic proportions in one of the world's largest chemical factories.

Town and factory grew up together, each sustaining the other. At first the company provided housing for its workers; it was accompanied from 1923 by the newly-formed Urban District Council (UDC) which had a wider remit. Private housing came later. The town expanded enormously in the inter-war years: from under 8,000 in 1921, its population grew to over 19,000 in the mid-1930s and to some 38,000 by the early 1970s. It is now around 33,500. The only direction possible for expansion was northward and, in due course, beyond the railway.

Growth was not haphazard. It was planned through the North Tees Joint Town Planning Scheme. Land was set aside for a town centre, although building was not begun until 1952. A new town in all but name, it was not one of those created under the New Towns Act of 1947. Of earlier origin, it adhered throughout to the ideals of the Garden City movement. Funded to a considerable extent from ICI's rateable value and fired by an enthusiastic Town Clerk and Council, Billingham pioneered the country's first District Heating Scheme, first combined Sport and Leisure Centre, first College of Further Education and first Campus Schools, an integrated educational project. Both the UDC and ICI encouraged and provided for sport and leisure. These were halcyon days, when the arts, theatre and music flourished, national names came to Billingham, and its International Folk Festival each summer drew, and still draws, dance groups from all over the world.

This album of 230 archive photographs aims to show something of life and work in Billingham from around the end of the nineteenth and the begining of the twentieth centuries to the 1970s. My interest in Billingham stems from my fascination in the way places evolve. In addition, my husband Kenneth has spent all his working life with ICI as a research chemist at Manchester and a patent attorney at Billingham. I thank him for his help, but absolve him from any mistakes I may have made in its preparation.

One

Billingham Village, Haverton Hill and Port Clarence

BILLINGHAM GREEN c. 1910. The place-name of this 'settlement of Billa's people' in the historic County of Durham is probably older than the seventh century. Until the end of the First World War, the village itself was still largely a rural community. The tall chimney of Heslop's Brewery was demolished in 1937. Few old buildings are now left.

Left: ST CUTHBERT'S SAXON CHURCH. The tall Saxon tower, a prominent landmark overlooking the Billingham Beck valley and by-pass, has belfry openings with unusual circles or stars. The tower was added c. 1000 AD to a long, high and narrow nave possibly dating from the late seventh or early eighth century. The nave walls were pierced to add aisles in the twelfth and thirteenth centuries and the tower raised a little in the fifteenth. Fragments of Saxon cross shafts were built into this remarkable building.

Below: THE SCHOOL ON THE GREEN. The stone plaques read, 'National School 1852' and 'pro Deo et ecclesia'. This Church of England school, enlarged in 1912 to take over 200 children, has been demolished and replaced by Prior's Mill School. (See page 85.)

Above: THE VILLAGE FROM THE CHURCH TOWER. Small houses surrounded the green. The lych gate of 1883 replaced five cottages. Tower House obscures the school, and beside it is the Shap granite cross of 1893, instigated by the vicar, the Revd Phillip Rudd. Chilton's Lane veers to the right, past the Chilton Estate houses and Chilton House old Main Offices (1927) and leads into the ICI Works where it was renamed Nitrates Avenue. Belasis Lane (now Avenue) veers away towards the left where later were built the Police Station, Billingham South School, the Public Baths, ICI Agricultural Division Offices (1959), the Synthonia Club and the tall chimneys of the Steam Reformers.

Right: CHAMPION PLOUGHMAN. John Dixon and his son Tom, at Glebe Farm, Chapel Road, from 1904, were widely known and are still remembered for their ploughing prowess and their horse and cart milk round. John Dixon began competing in 1895, won his first open ploughing championship at 19, and by the age of 29 had won over 200 prizes, including 100 firsts.

CHILTON'S LANE, 1922. This lane led to Billingham Grange Farm, Tibbersley Farm and Haverton Hill. It was partly dismantled to allow the chemical works to spread over these two farmlands. By 1925 the New Road was built to the south as a replacement.

THE GRANGE FARMHOUSE, built c. 1760 (see page 91). The medieval open fields of Billingham – the Milne Field, Middle Field and North Field – were enclosed in 1617. Peasant farms could then move away from the village. There were also three independent medieval farms: Belasis, granted by William the Conqueror to his knight de Belasis, was moated; Beaulieu, also moated, was the Prior of Durham's 'beautiful place', where he held feasts and a manor court (see page 13); Saltholme, beside the Tees estuary marshes, came in the fourteenth century.

LOW GRANGE FARMHOUSE (BEAULIEU) UNDER DEMOLITION, 1964. Decayed by the seventeenth century and bombed in the Second World War, part was still a farmhouse identified by excavation in 1960-61 as Beaulieu. Two buildings were discovered. The older, perhaps a fortified tower, remained only as foundation walls six feet wide. Joined at one corner was a storeroom beneath a lancet-windowed first-floor hall, identified as the manor house built by Prior Hugh in the thirteenth century. Traces of its fish pond and watermill were found. (Leslie Still)

BILLINGHAM WATERMILL. The mill at tidal limit on Billingham Beck was reached from the village via Mill Lane, a path and a footbridge. The buildings date from c. 1710. The mill was worked by the Moon family from the 1870s until c. 1905, briefly reopening in 1914-1929. The house became a farmworker's dwelling for nearby Brook House Farm, whose land from 1930 became ICI South Works (now Cassel Works), where sodium, sodium cyanide, caustic soda and chlorine were produced.

NORTON WATERMILL, c.1885. This early photograph shows the East and West Mills, the mill house and the Watson family. The Watsons moved from Wolviston Mill to Norton Mill in 1870. They worked it until closure in 1920, using steam from 1915. The Watsons owned both Norton and Billingham Mills, but Norton Mill was taken over by miller Skelton who married one of the Watson girls c. 1900. Bombed in 1940, the mill was levelled in 1947, and the site excavated in 1978 in advance of the A19 by-pass.

THE WATSON GIRLS OF NORTON MILL, born at the mill c. 1880s. Mill Lane now ends at the new roundabout on the A19 bypass. The mill site is now in Billingham Beck Valley Country Park and Ecology Park. This freshwater wetland has 150 types of wild flowers, a lake for pond-dipping, a summer cornfield meadow with poppies, cornflowers and golden corn marigolds, a limestone rockery and planted woodland.

WOLVISTON MILL, 1890s. Also powered by Billingham Beck, the mill ceased operation around 1870. The water wheel is encased in brick on the left. Mrs Peacock, born a Watson, is in the garden. She died in 1931 aged about 94. The mill was bombed in 1940, sold by auction in 1973 and burnt down in 1974, the last mill on the Beck and its tributaries to retain its wheel and machinery intact.

NORTON GREEN POND. A quiet rural scene with pond and pump – intruded upon by gas lamps and an electric tram from around 1897. Norton was to grow greatly with the coming of Billingham industry, and ICI's Norton Hall staff club and visitor accommodation now faces the main green.

BELASIS VILLAGE, 1918. The eight-berth Furness Shipyard was built beside the Tees at Haverton Hill in 1917-18 to replace ships sunk during the First World War. The first ship was launched in 1919. Lord Furness built a model village for his workforce, seen here nearing completion in December 1918. A total of 531 houses was built in 438 days near Belasis Farm (see page 12), itself destroyed by bombing in the Second World War.

HAVERTON HILL BOYS' SCHOOL, c. 1953. The teachers are Miss Margaret Poulton and Les Jobson. The school has been demolished.

HAVERTON HILL BOYS' SCHOOL, c. 1954, which went mixed c. 1958 and has since been demolished.

BELASIS AVENUE, HAVERTON HILL, 1964. Downwind from the ICI cement plant and covered in dust, Lord Furness's model village (see page 16) was soon to be demolished. (Vera Chapman)

PORT CLARENCE: ST THOMAS' SENIOR SCHOOL, 1948-49. Mr J.L. Carter was the headmaster from 1947 to 1954. This, the first Roman Catholic school in the Billingham area, was built in 1880 and closed in 1978. St Gerard's School was built twenty years later at Belasis Hill to relieve the pressure here.

ST THOMAS'S SENIOR FOOTBALL TEAM, 1948-49. The Clarence Railway, named c. 1828 after the Duke of Clarence (later William IV), opened in 1833 to serve coal staithes on the River Tees at Samphire Batts, renamed Port Clarence. Bell Brothers' ironworks came in 1853, followed by housing and schools.

Above: BELL STREET, PORT CLARENCE. St Thomas of Canterbury's church and school are at the end. Father Burke was responsible for their being built. The toddler is Kathleen, one of the seven children of Donny Fairweather, now Mrs Smith and a grandmother. She recalls allotments at the end of Bell Street, and men's leisure at Morley's Station Hotel.

Right: TERESA, JEAN AND WINNIE FAIRWEATHER, 1944.

GREATHAM SALTWELLS DERRICK, 1965. A bed of rock salt around 1,000 ft underground was discovered in 1874 and developed by Bell Brothers. Salt was used for caustic soda and chlorine. Port Clarence and Haverton Hill became ringed with saltwell pumps for brine extraction. In the 1880s there were five saltworks. Cerebos ended operations in the 1970s. Salt had been worked at Cowpen in the thirteenth and fourteenth centuries, and near Redcar mounds from sea salt panning remained until recently. (Tom Hay)

TRANSPORTER BRIDGE, PORT CLARENCE, 1960. Built in 1911 by the Cleveland Bridge and Engineering Company, it replaced a Tees ferry upstream of the coal staithes and eased access to Middlesbrough. Dramatic and graceful despite its size, cars and pedestrians are carried on a platform slung by cables from a gantry some 200 ft above the river. The buildings on the right have now gone. (Vera Chapman)

Two

Billingham between the Wars

MILL LANE HOUSES UNDER CONSTRUCTION, early 1920s. Seventy-eight four-bedroomed semis were built in Mill Lane by the Synthetic Ammonia and Nitrates Company (forerunners of ICI) to house the key workers who set up production.

A MILL LANE PAIR NEARING COMPLETION. More 'Synthetic' housing was built in the Roscoe Road area in rows of four, followed by a further 200 houses by the North East Housing Association. Mill Lane shops and a cinema came in 1928.

CRESCENT HOUSING, 1936. Housing estates in crescent form are characteristic of inter-war Billingham. The Chilton Estate (1924-26) was followed northward by the Belasis Estate astride Central Avenue. The Cowpen Lane and Pentland Avenue Estates continued beyond the Clarence Railway (see page 25). By 1935 'the Synthetic' and ICI had built 2,000 houses for its own workforce, and the UDC, formed in 1923 with a wider responsibility, had completed 1,100. Billingham's population grew from 8,000 in 1921 to 19,000 in 1935.

THE CO-OP. The Stockton and District Society's branch on Belasis Lane corner is now a car showroom above which the former Synthonia Players perform as Theatre Upstairs. The lawn on the right, on Mill Lane corner, replaces a sunken garden, lily pool, chalet and seats. The cinema on the other corner of Mill Lane is also now a car showroom.

STATION ROAD. Shopping and private housing developed along Station Road in the early inter-war years, developed by Scotson of Wolviston. The Station Road by-pass was built in 1943 and opened in 1944 to relieve the level crossing bottleneck. (Courtesy The Francis Frith Collection)

BILLINGHAM SOUTH SCHOOL. Schools had to be built for the families flooding in to serve the burgeoning ICI. This large school on Belasis Avenue opened in 1929. The linking walkways have been removed. (From a painting by C.F. Mouncey)

PUPILS IN HAPPY MOOD, Billingham South School assembly hall.

AERIAL VIEW ALONG CENTRAL AVENUE. The view extends eastwards from the Station Road by-pass, over Station Road, across ICI-built Belasis Estate with (mainly) Dales street names, to Cowpen Lane. From left to right across the top of the photograph are Charlton's Pond, football ground, Roseberry Bridge (1954) over the LNER Port Clarence Branch, St John's school and church, ICI new Main Offices, the Public Baths, Billingham South School and ICI Works. Jean Watson has lived in Central Avenue since 1931, and remembers playing whip and top and skipping on Central Avenue – no cars then; only the surges of ICI workers on bicycles! (Photograph by Turners Photography)

PROCESSION, CENTRAL AVENUE, 1933. It wound from Billingham village green via Central Avenue to the opening of the new St John the Evangelist RC school on Cowpen Lane. Just behind the banner and carrying a candle is Ken Bradley, now aged 70. (*Evening Gazette*, Teesside)

ST JOHN THE EVANGELIST PRESBYTERY AND SCHOOL. Bishop Thorman, Bishop of Hexham and Newcastle, laid the school foundation stone. This all-age school opened in 1933, the ceremony being followed by children's sports and prizes, with Father E.J. Connell presiding. It became a Primary in 1964 when St Michael's Comprehensive opened.

ST JOHN'S SCHOOL HALL. This served also for social and religious purposes until the new church was opened on an adjoining site (see page 30). A screen is drawn back to make a sanctuary and small chapel.

'JAN OF WINDMILL HILL', 1933. The children's concert group poses outside St John's School.

INFANT 2 CLASS, ST JOHN'S SCHOOL.

FORM 2A, ST JOHN'S SCHOOL.

PREFECTS, ST JOHN'S SCHOOL.

ST JOHN'S STAFF, APRIL 1961.

ST JOHN'S NETBALL 'A' TEAM, 1961.

ST JOHN'S RC CHURCH. Built 1959-61, it was opened on 7 June 1961.

CHOIR BOYS of St John's church.

PILGRIMAGE. St John's and probably members of other churches set off for Lourdes, 3 June 1957.

NINETIETH BIRTHDAYS of Annie Mortimer and Monica Mansell were recently celebrated at St John's, with Father David Taylor presiding.

THE WENDY HOUSE, 5 FEBRUARY 1943. Note the gas masks hanging beneath the tables! This photograph by Miss S. Roxby, the first headmistress, was sent by her to Anne Springett. Billingham North School was officially opened for infants in June 1938 by County Councillor A.T.S. Zealley, managing director of ICI Billingham, and for juniors in January 1941, with Miss Melrose as the first head. After growth and shrinkage, the two joined in 1980 to become Pentland Primary School under Mrs Anne Liddle.

BILLINGHAM NORTH SCHOOL. A semi-circular window was a feature in both school halls. The School Outings Book records a journey by train to Wensleydale on 23 June 1939, leaving Billingham at 11.06am, lunch on the train, via Aysgarth, arriving at Appleby LMS, departing from Appleby LNER, tea on the train, arriving Barnard Castle 7.01, departing at 8.45 and arriving at Billingham at 9.55pm. Excavations in progress at Piercebridge Roman fort were noted.

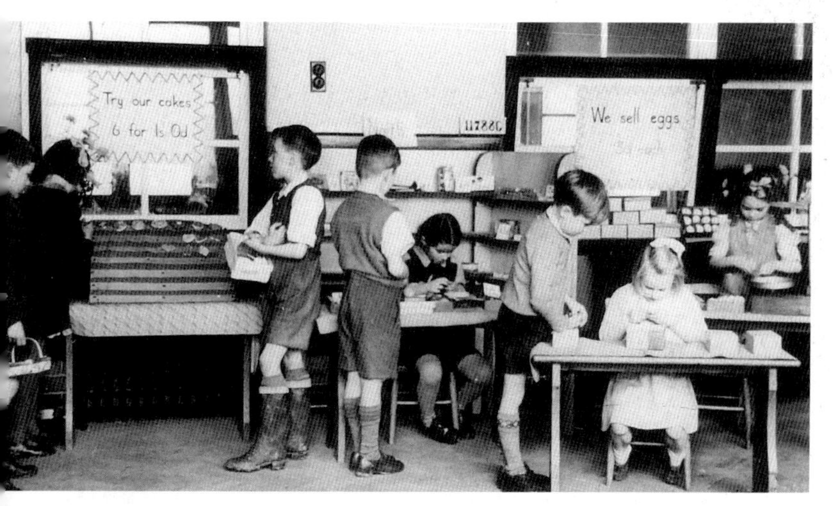

PLAYING SHOP: PRACTICAL MATHEMATICS. The golden jubilee celebrations of Billingham North, now Pentland School, were attended by Dr Keith Farmery, operations manager for ICI Chemicals and Polymers in Billingham.

HARVEST FESTIVAL. Billingham North (Pentland) School puts on a display in one of the semi-circular windows.

A SPECIAL OCCASION. Pentland Primary School children celebrate – but what?

Three

Around the New Town Centre

THE TOWN CENTRE: AN EARLY STAGE. Roseberry Road is at the bottom right. The Causeway swings past the library and health centre, the new community centre, Stockton-Billingham Technical College, John Whitehead Park and the Billingham Arms Hotel. Access remained by road past the north row of shops and through the East Precinct. The vacant ground beyond has yet to receive the Civic Buildings, Kennedy Gardens flats and the Forum.

Left: CORONATION CELEBRATIONS, 1952. The first prize for a decorated street, Richmond Crescent, was presented by Councillor Dudley Chapman, Chairman of Billingham UDC, to Mr and Mrs Les and Ethel Jobson.

Below: BILLINGHAM NORTH END FOOTBALL CLUB, c. 1952. The team played, firstly, on the field which became Roseberry Schools, then on the site where the District Heating Boiler House is now, then on the field where the Forum was built in 1967. After this the club amalgamated with the nearby Working Men's Club team. (Reproduced with the permission of the *Hartlepool Mail*)

AT THE OLD COMMUNITY CENTRE, 1958. Here are Lord Lawson of Beamish (Jack Lawson, National Union of Mineworkers), Councillors J. Ramsay and D. Chapman, Ernest Jobson (on the left) and, on the far right, Mr Calvert, the Warden.

OVER-60s CHOIR, c. 1965. The conductor is Vin Brown, centre. On the back row are the pianist Amy Watson and Councillor Mrs McClean; on the far right of the front row is Mrs Barbara Jobson.

THE TOWN CENTRE AT A LATER STAGE. Another shopping row has been built with a spiral ramp to an upper deck. The central mall is now pedestrianized. Beyond (westward) is vacant ground and in the distance are the houses along Roseberry Road.

THE TOWN CENTRE, 1964. Looking westward from the spiral ramp is an art exhibition kiosk, the former road and the vacant ground upon which a two-decker shopping development will later be built. Beyond is the health centre and library. (Vera Chapman)

THE TOWN CENTRE. The two-decker shops with flats above were begun in 1962. Behind these shops was a parallel row of two-tier parking decks, the upper one linked to the shops by bridges over a rear service road. (The Teesside Industrial Development Board)

AERIAL VIEW, TOWN CENTRE, looking north-west. The new parking decks and shops and the pedestrian mall are in the foreground. Beyond is The Causeway and, from the left, Sidlaw Road, the new Community Centre, the Technical College with its theatre, Finchale Road and the bowling greens in John Whitehead Park. (UDC)

TOWN CENTRE, January 1964, looking north-east. Father Christmas still rides above the exhibition kiosk. Amenities are not yet complete. Ken Bates remembers that for a while there were bird cages, and that mannequins from an upper deck dress shop paraded down the spiral ramp.

AMENITIES COMPLETED. Looking east, the Kennedy Gardens high-rise flats loom in the distance beyond the East Precinct.

Right: KENNEDY GARDENS. Three tower blocks of flats were completed in the town centre in 1962. Each flat was individually metered for heat from a district heating system. (NCB)

Below: BILLINGHAM GROUP HEATING SCHEME: THE BOILER HOUSE. This was sited beside Marsh House Avenue, near the town centre. The NCB solid fuel district heating scheme served the town centre and thirty acres of light industry. The fuel, washed singles, was delivered pneumatically via couplings to high level bunkers. It was the first such scheme in the country, and in 1966 the UDC was awarded the NALGO 'Accolade for Enterprise'. The plant is now run by AHS Emstar Energy Management. (NCB)

CONDUCTED TOUR, c. 1963-64. In the East Precinct are, from the left, Fred Dawson (Clerk to the UDC) (see pages 2 and 43), Keith Joseph MP, Councillors Maureen Taylor (now MBE, JP) and Robert (Bob) Duncan, with Bill Rodgers MP behind. (*Evening Gazette*, Teesside)

HRH THE DUKE OF EDINBURGH'S VISIT. Councillor Bob Duncan was the Chairman of the UDC. The Duke came alone and did tree planting. (UDC)

HM QUEEN ELIZABETH'S VISIT, 1967. Her Majesty, accompanied by HRH The Prince Philip, opened the Tyne Tunnel, then travelled by train to Billingham. Escorted by UDC chairman Douglas Turnbull, she unveiled the Family Group statue by Bainbridge Copnall which represents the spirit of the town. After opening The Forum, she continued to Darlington for its Borough Centenary celebrations. Fred Dawson OBE, here being presented, began as a junior clerk at Tynemouth and served for twenty years as the clerk to Billingham UDC. In 1967 he became the director of the North East Development Council and retired in 1972. He died in 1988.

HM THE QUEEN'S VISIT. HRH The Prince Philip, The Duke of Edinburgh, greets town dignitaries. Mrs Irene (Rene) Dawson is on the right.

CHARLTON'S POND, 1974. This former clay pit off Cowpen Lane was designated a bird sanctuary in 1966 and is managed by Cleveland Wildlife Trust. In nearby Lincoln Crescent a plaque records trees planted in May 1937 for the Coronation of King George VI. The chimneys were for ICI Agricultural Division's four steam reforming plants. After further processes ammonia, fertilizers and Drikold resulted (see page 98). Two old cooling towers behind the central chimneys were nicknamed Gert and Daisy, after two stage comediennes. The solitary cooling tower is a legacy of the 1920s, when coal was the feedstock.

ROSEBERRY INFANTS, 1977. The teacher is Mrs Blissett. The infant school beyond The Causeway was formally opened in 1955 by County Councillor W. Dent. It was to serve the Roseberry Estate of 1,500 houses which recommenced the northward development of the town beyond the railway.

ROSEBERRY INFANTS, c. 1970s. Philip Forrester and friends are dressed up, probably for Christmas.

AT THEIR DESKS, c. 1970s. Roseberry infants pause from their work.

THE SAND TRAY, c. 1970s. Roseberry infants are, from the left, David Mattison, Stephen Duck, David Fleet and Glen Fleet.

CHRISTMAS FAIRIES, c. 1970s. Roseberry infants line up.

ROSEBERRY JUNIOR SCHOOL, 1958-59. The football team with teachers (left to right) W. Jewitt, L. Stribling, I. Archer and L. Jobson.

ROSEBERRY JUNIORS, 1958.

STAFF GROUP, April 1959. Roseberry Junior School teachers are, from the left, back row: L. Jobson, K. McQueen, Jean Bell, -?-, E. Kennedy and I. Archer. Front row: -?-, L. Stribling, W. Jewitt (head), Dorothy Arnold and Mrs Golightly.

SPEECH DAY, 1959. Roseberry Junior School pupils on the front row are, from the left, Susan Hayes, -?-, Margaret Jobson, Linda Heppell, Carol Turner and Brenda Dickinson. On the right, at the back, is Mrs Ethel Jobson. Margaret Jobson, now Mrs Halliwell, was at the school from its opening in 1957. She remembers its first head, Mr Jewitt, and staff members Mr Archer, Mr O'Neill and Mrs Golightly. (See page 66)

GYMNASTICS TEAM, Roseberry Junior School, 1983.

SWIMMING TEAM, Roseberry Junior School, 1983.

ROAD SAFETY QUIZ TEAM, Roseberry Junior School, 1983.

UPPER AND LOWER MUSICIANS, Roseberry Juniors, 1984.

BILLINGHAM TECHNICAL COLLEGE. The College beside The Causeway was the second phase of Stockton Technical College. It was Durham County Council's first College of Further Education, claimed to be one of the first in Britain. Opened in 1958, it is soon to be moved to a new site in Stockton. Staff seen here are thought to include Len Law, David Bimson, George Scratcherd, Peter Hardwick, John Mitchell, Edna Reddy, David Garrood, John Beadle, Glen Watson, Margaret Dorn, Jack Patterson, D.E. Scripts, Eddie Moore, Maurice Critchley, Neville Kale, Neville Oneless, Val Lister, Kathleen Terry and Maureen Bates.

BILLINGHAM TECHNICAL COLLEGE. On the left is Alan Oyston, former vice-principal and then principal, and on the right Ted Griffin, head of engineering and later vice-principal, with two engineering students and their awards.

SIR MORTIMER WHEELER, 1958. Prior to his lecture in the Technical College theatre the famous archaeologist is greeting Miss Margaret Baxter (Secretary of the college archaeological society) and Mr Alec Murray (Vice-Chairman of the Students' Union). Wheeler directed a post-war excavation at the Brigantian earthworks at Stanwick, near Scotch Corner.

THE COLLEGE LIBRARY. Eva O'Boyle is busy at the catalogues.

Four

The Forum: Sport, Theatre and International Festival

THE FORUM. Built in 1965-67 and opened by HM The Queen, this showpiece Forum housed together for the first time a variety of activities. It set a precedent for leisure centres throughout Britain, and was designed by Elder, Lester and Partners. The ice-rink on the left has a suspended roof, a concave tensile structure on diagonal beams.

WOULD-BE SWIMMERS. A teaching class at the learners' pool is ready to go.

ARCHERY in the multi-purpose hall.

RHYTHMIC MOVEMENT.

SQUASH.

BOY'S JUDO CLASS.

WEIGHT TRAINING.

Right: SKATING CHAMPION. Joanne Hall, then a second year pupil at St Michael's RC Comprehensive School, was the North-East Junior Skating Champion, and won the free skating section of the Sunderland Open Competition. Neil and Lisa Cushley became international skaters, representing Britain abroad.

Below: GYMNASTICS. A teaching class in progress.

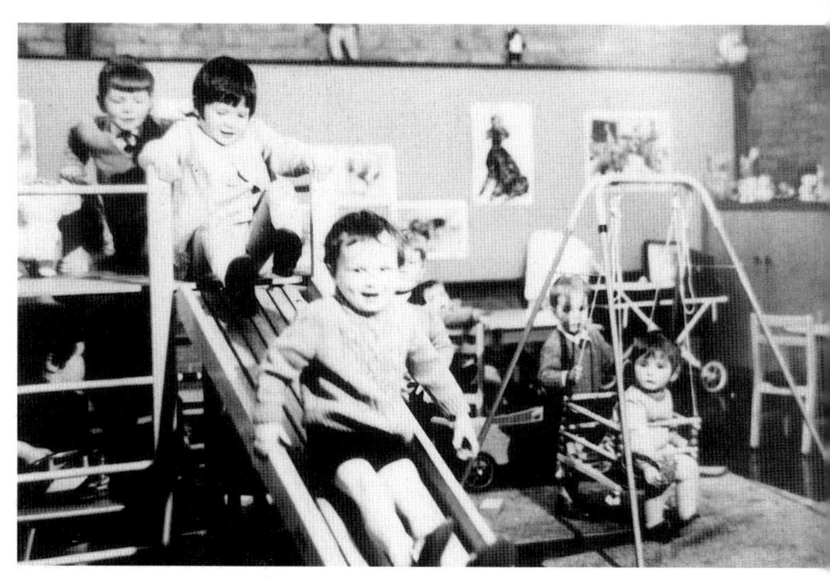

THE CRECHE.

INAUGURATION OF THE THEATRE. Councillor John Scott in the Sports Hall after the ceremony in the theatre.

THE FORUM THEATRE INTERIOR. The vertical walls and box fronts are timber clad.

LES JOBSON AND TIMOTHY WEST. Les was the first manager of the theatre. Employed at ICI's analytical laboratory before the war, he ferried Catalina Flying Boats to Ceylon during the Second World War, then taught in Billingham schools for twenty years. He was the *Express* music critic and Secretary of the Billingham Arts Association and Billingham Entertainments Committee. Timothy West 'arrived one day' and directed productions. He recently played Winston Churchill in a TV series.

A FORUM STAGE SET for a *Dick Whittington* pantomime at the Globe Theatre, Stockton. Whilst Les Jobson was manager, the Forum workshops made stage sets and costumes for its own shows and sold them on to other companies. The theatre produced fifteen shows that went on to the West End, and fifty that went on national tours. This and the following four photographs are examples of the Forum workshops' achievements.

THE KING AND I. A 1970s rehearsal in progress. Sally Ann Howes plays Anna.

ANN RODGERS IN *QUADRILLE*, 1977.

MARGARET LOCKWOOD AND ALFRED HOFFMAN IN *QUADRILLE*, 1977.

RICHARD TODD IN *QUADRILLE*, 1977.

ANNA NEAGLE PLAYED IN *MAGGIE*, 1977, which went on to the West End.

ARTHUR LOWE at a garden party in Hart village.

PENELOPE KEITH AND NIGEL HAWTHORNE, now best known for *To the Manor Born* and *Yes, Minister*.

DAVID JASON. His photograph is inscribed 'For Les and Jean. Thanks for a really super show and very happy stay. Can I come again please?'

OWEN BRANNIGAN, a baritone well known for his Tyneside songs. Others who came to Billingham included Ernest Lush, Max Bygraves and the Max Jaffa Trio. Music and the arts were active in the growing town, even before the Forum was built. Artistes on tour could economically perform at Billingham after Newcastle.

DOBSON AND YOUNG 'TALKING ABOUT MUSIC', 1950s. These two professors (not of music) at Manchester University gave shows in their spare time. The first concert ever given in Billingham was held in the College Theatre in 1962, when the BBC Northern Orchestra played Dvorak's *Carnival Overture*, a Mozart symphony, Hindersmith's *Mathis de Maler* and Rimsky-Korsakov's *Scheherezade*. World renowned orchestras on tour came to Billingham from, for example, Munich, Berlin and Leipzig.

LES JOBSON AND THE BILLINGHAM INTERNATIONAL FOLKLORE FESTIVAL. The Festival began in 1965, a two-day weekend event in the John Whitehead Park. It rained!

ROQUE NUBLO, CANARY ISLANDS, 1966. In its second year the Festival really 'took off', with the Canaries group and an Irish group.

THE FESTIVAL, 1967. Les Jobson's daughter Margaret, at the front of a procession along The Causeway (see page 48), interpreted for a German group. Margaret, now Mrs Halliwell, runs several language schools in Germany.

FOLK DANCE ENSEMBLE 'VARNA', FROM BULGARIA.

BRIGHAM YOUNG UNIVERSITY FOLK DANCERS, 1974. They came from the Salt Lake City area and were touring Europe. The women wore scarlet, the men turquoise blue. The Red Indian headdress feathers were also blue.

NORTH VANCOUVER YOUTH BAND, BRITISH COLUMBIA, 1975. The musical director of this large band was Arthur Smith.

Five

Northward Expansion: Schools of the Sixties and Seventies

LOW GRANGE JUNIORS. The school began in 1959 and was formally opened in 1960 by Mrs E. Clennell. Standing on the right at the rear is Susan Long, now Mrs Gordon, whose own child Louise Gordon is now in the junior school, having started in the infants school.

LOW GRANGE JUNIORS. These original school furnishings of 1959 have now been replaced. The three-form entry school catered for the Low Grange Estate then being built on Radburn Plan principles which separated houses from traffic (see page 13). The junior school has had only three head teachers in its thirty-seven years: George William Gale 1959-73, Brian W. Docherty 1973-1991 and Michael Tennant. The junior and infant schools, with separate buildings and head teachers, were to provide 840 places.

LOW GRANGE JUNIOR STAFF, c. 1962. Front row, from the left: -?-, -?-, Les Jobson (deputy head), George Gale (head), Miss Carpenter, Desmond Carroll and Margaret Allen.

LOW GRANGE INFANTS, 1976. The Christmas nativity tableau. The infants' department was ready in 1960 and was formally opened in 1961 by County Councillor Mrs S. Shaw.

LOW GRANGE INFANTS STAFF, 1984. From the left, back row: Miss J. Richardson, Mrs O'Connor, Mrs Lowther, Mrs Cummins, Mrs Martin. Front row: Mrs Harrison, Ms Yeomans, Mrs Bainbridge, Mrs Todd (head), Mrs Kellety (deputy head), Mrs Devereux, Mrs Sutherland.

POND DIPPING, 1988. Low Grange infants use their nets.

BEDE HALL SCHOOL. Mr Brian Appleby, far right, is teaching basic canoeing skills. In the canoes, from the left, are Janet Bolton, John Fawcett, Margaret Wrightson, Pauline Sedgewick, Paul Ferguson and Stephen Harvey. Two senior pupils help to keep the canoes steady. School clubs included swimming, table tennis, soccer, cricket, netball, tennis, folk and Outward Bound.

CAMPUS SCHOOLS, 1964. This integrated educational project began in 1958 with one secondary modern before the full scheme was approved. Built in 1960-62 to the designs of Middleton, Fletcher and Partners for 2,000 pupils, it consisted of three secondary moderns and one grammar-technical on one site. There were sciences and practical subjects in one block and PE in another. The whole was reorganized in 1972 into comprehensives and a sixth form college. (Vera Chapman)

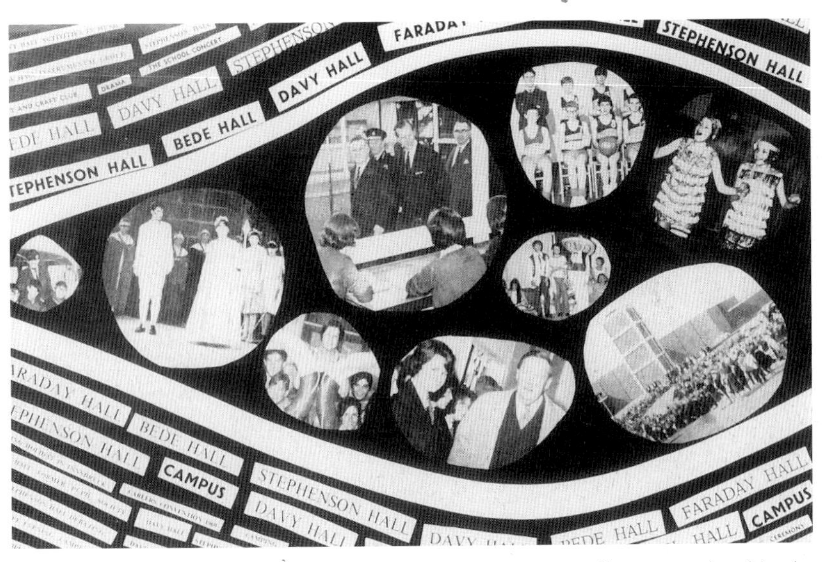

CAMPUS SCHOOLS. A booklet containing this commemorative collage was produced for the 1972 reorganization.

Left: HOCKEY INTERNATIONAL MRS ANNE WHITWORTH was head of PE in Bede Hall School on the Campus. She played for England as far afield as New Zealand and USA.

Below: ST MICHAEL'S RC COMPREHENSIVE, 1960s. The school's first ever action picture is of the drama group. The school uniform was a black blazer and grey flannels for the boys, and a grey blazer and grey skirt for the girls. St Michael's opened in 1964, enabling the earlier all-age RC schools to become primaries. St Joseph's opened in 1968 and St Paul's in 1970, relieving Holy Rosary School and reflecting town expansion.

Above: ST MICHAEL'S FIRST HEAD TEACHER, 1976. Mr Eddie Payne, seen here with a class of that date, was the head from 1964-76. He died in 1995.

Right: MUSICIAN ELENA DE JESUS, a pupil at St Michael's, was a member of the National Children's Orchestra of Great Britain. She played at concerts at the Queen Elizabeth Hall in London, in York and at Huddersfield, and was presented to HRH The Princess of Wales after a concert in St David's Hall, Cardiff. She also played with an ensemble on BBC TV's 'Breakfast Time' programme.

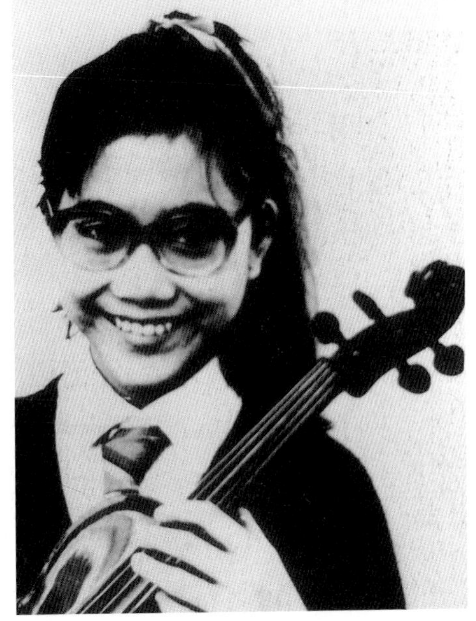

IT'S A KNOCK OUT. This programme and competition was very popular at St Michael's in the 1970s.

CROSS-COUNTRY RUN, c. 1977. St Michael's upper school pupils are eager to set off.

FOOTBALLERS. England Under-21 international footballer Jamie Pollock (centre) captained the St Michael's team which, in 1990, reached the quarter-finals of the English Schools Cup. He now plays for Middlesbrough. Also pictured, on the left of the back row, is Sean Gregan who now plays for Darlington. The trophy is the Cleveland County Shield, which dates from the time of the Boer War.

JAMIE POLLOCK recently visited St Michael's for its Fancy Hats charity day.

STAFF, ST MICHAEL'S SCHOOL, c. 1988. From the left are G.A. Maxwell, deputy head (now head), V.G. Shanley (head), and Mrs E.M. Early, senior mistress.

BEWLEY JUNIOR SCHOOL. To celebrate its twenty-fifth anniversary in 1991 there was a great dressing up! Entering into the spirit are dinner ladies, left to right, Lilian Benson, Dot Cook, Val Stelling, Sue Newman, Mrs Elstob, Maureen Tuft and Karen Jones. Les Jobson was the first head, followed by Norman Brookes, who has recently retired.

BEWLEY JUNIORS, RED NOSE DAY, 1988. The Cleveland Community Forest has been planted across the road from the school grounds. Bewley Juniors helped with the planting, and an exhibition about the project was held in the school. (Margaret Rees)

CHRISTMAS CONCERT, 1988. Bewley juniors are singing. (Margaret Rees)

'WE MAKE MUSICAL INSTRUMENTS.' A Bewley junior class in progress. (Margaret Rees)

ST JOSEPH'S RC PRIMARY SCHOOL. Miss Killick conducts music in the school hall in the early 1970s. Competitions were entered at Whitby and elsewhere. The school opened in 1967.

A FIRST COMMUNION, c. 1980. With the seven-year-olds are Mrs McTimoney, left, and Mr Bradley, right.

EASTER BONNETS, 1981, an annual feature at St Joseph's for many years.

ST JOSEPH'S STAFF, 1971. From the left, back row: Miss Fields, Miss Reid, Miss Killick, Mrs McTimoney, Mrs Wells, Mrs O'Connor. Front row: Mr O'Connor, Mrs Romeanes, Mr Bradley, Mrs Meridith, Mr Lamb.

THE SCHOOL LIBRARY, early 1970s. St Joseph's opened in 1967.

THE REVD FATHER WILFRED ARROWSMITH, the first parish priest of St Joseph's, 1962-1976.

THE REVD FATHER DAVID HEAD, the parish priest of St Joseph's 1976-1990. The new RC church was opened c. 1981.

ST PAUL'S RC PRIMARY SCHOOL, 1971. The school opened in 1968, on the edge of the Wolviston Court Estate. These seven-year-olds take their first communion.

ST PAUL'S FOOTBALL TEAM, 1979-80. The team wore red jerseys and socks and the 'goalie' wore blue.

Right: THE RT REVD THE LORD BISHOP OF DURHAM. Dr Ian T. Ramsey was Bishop of Durham 1966-72, and in 1970 became the chairman of a national commission on religious education in schools. He officially opened Billingham C. of E. (Controlled) Junior School in Clifton Avenue in 1971. It joined Northfield Infants' School, which had opened on the site in 1968, and took pupils from 1970 under its first head Mr J. Ison. The old school on Billingham Green was then demolished (see page 10).

Below: PRIOR'S MILL SCHOOL DINING AREA, 1971. The name of the new C. of E. school was chosen by pupils, parents and governors. It appropriately linked the Prior of Durham, who owned Billingham Mill, with the people who lived in the Northfield area and would have ground their corn at that mill (see page 13).

PRIOR'S MILL SCHOOL, 1971. Junior mathematics is in progress.

THE ACTIVITY AREA, 1971. Art work in progress at Prior's Mill School.

Six

ICI – The Early Years

Start-up, Products, Oil-from-Coal and Transport

TRANSITION, 1918. Mr D.L. White was employed by the site owners, the Ministry of Munitions for War. When he retired in 1935 he was cashier for ICI Billingham. In the background are the Grange farmhouse and wooden offices.

THE SITE, JANUARY 1922. The munitions factory was set up during the First World War to make synthetic nitrates for explosives, by way of replacement for Chilean nitrates lost at sea to enemy action. In 1919 the unfinished site was taken over by Brunner Mond. In 1920 the Synthetic Ammonia and Nitrates Company was formed to make fertilizers. This view shows tall storage tanks, and railway tracks installed for construction traffic and supplies.

THE FIRST TRAFFIC DEPARTMENT. These huts beside the factory entrance had been used by the Ministry. The Grange farmhouse garden is to the right.

THE FIRST LORRY, 1926. Synthetic Ammonia and Nitrates Ltd merged to become a part of Imperial Chemical Industries Ltd in 1926.

ANOTHER 'SYNTHETIC' LORRY, post-1926. Note that the ICI Ltd name has been added in two places. The lorry has solid tyres and was perhaps a Scammell.

LABORATORIES, 1922, the first permanent buildings to be erected.

EARLY WORKERS. Second from the left is F.M. Ray.

STAFF GROUP which includes J. Dixon Smith on the left and C.S. Guthrie second from the right.

THE GRANGE FARMHOUSE. Built c. 1760 and bereft of its land for industrial use, it survived until recent times, colour-washed, converted, extended and completely hemmed in by ICI plant.

TANKER LORRY, c. 1930. This 'Commercial Works' lorry has pneumatic tyres and the characteristic hub caps of an AEC.

STORAGE AND HANDLING.

SOUTH SITE - CASSEL WORKS.

SOUTH SITE - CASSEL WORKS (see page 6).

ANHYDRITE MINE. From 1923 a bed of anhydrite over 30 ft thick was mined by Casebourne Works from a shaft around 800 ft deep. It was reacted with ammonium carbonate to give ammonium sulphate (previously obtained from gasworks) for use as fertilizer. Other uses of anhydrite were in making wall plaster, plasterboard, cement and sulphuric acid.

ANHYDRITE MINERS TRAVELLING TO THE WORKFACE. Eventually there were one and a half square miles of workings underneath the ICI site. The mine closed in 1971.

PARABOLIC SILO. In this vast air-conditioned concrete silo, sulphate of ammonia cascades from conveyor bands in the roof. The storage capacity is about 100,000 tons. The amount in store varies seasonally with the demands of agriculture. Products Works produced over a million tons of fertilizers a year – sulphate of ammonia, Nitro-Chalk and CCF (Compound Complete Fertiliser).

PACKAGING. Measuring and weighing sodium cyanide pellets into drums. Such pellets were referred to as 'eggs' on ICI Blackley Works in Manchester.

BAGGED CEMENT BEING LOADED ONTO LORRIES, 1930s.

PACKAGING PLASTERBOARD. Production ceased in the 1960s.

PACKAGING FERTILIZER. It was despatched in bags to farmers and storage depots all over Britain.

Left: DRIKOLD, c. late 1930s. Drikold (a registered trade mark), or dry-ice refrigerant, is solid carbon dioxide, a by-product of making ammonia synthesis gas. Here it is being used as an ice-cream coolant.

Below: BAGGING MACHINE. Much equipment is manufactured in ICI's own workshops, including boxes, barrels, casks and drums, and items as large as wagons. Sacks and bags were made successively of jute, paper and plastic. The 'Big Bags' were so large and heavy that they had to be moved by crane.

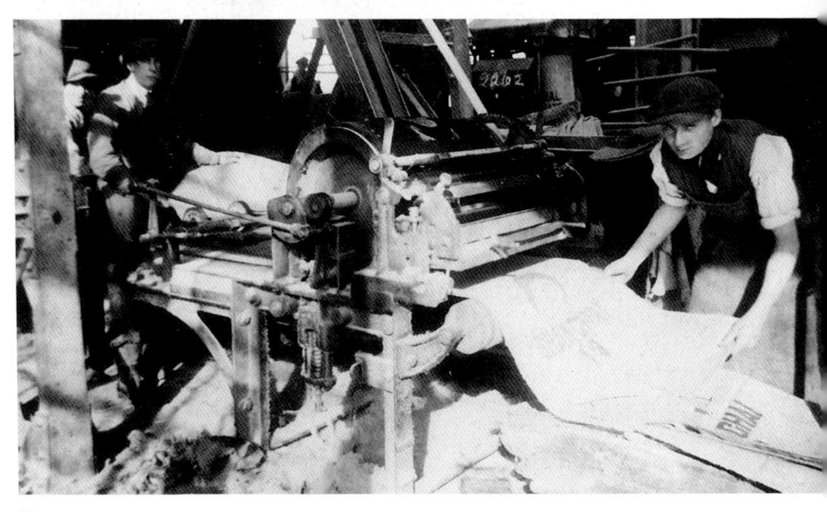

LOADING FERTILIZERS.

OIL WORKS SITE, 1934. Riverside petrol storage tanks under construction near New Road. Note the four workmen below the tanks platform on the left. The distant drift of smoke is from Middlesbrough ironmasters' district, where the last blast furnaces would be demolished in the 1960s. Making oil from coal was new technology, a pioneer project of economic and strategic importance. Being on a greenfield site, maintenance, storage, handling and transport services had to be built as well as the high-pressure coal-to-oil plant itself.

COAL-OIL PILOT PLANT, 1929. A pilot plant was built and started up during 1929. Here, a high-pressure converter is being installed, using a sledge on rollers. The scale and engineering of Oil Works at that time involved unique technology of heroic proportions.

COAL-OIL PILOT PLANT. A petrol rail tanker is being filled.

START OF THE FULL-SCALE PLANT, 1933. The site of the petrol plant viewed in September from the south-west, with a pipebridge in the background. Nine thousand workers were involved in the construction.

COOLING TOWER UNDER CONSTRUCTION next to the New Road, February 1934. The tower was for cooling the reaction products of the coal hydrogenation process. The completed tower appears in the next photograph.

THE TITAN CRANE, 1935. The travelling crane, a site landmark, was built in 1933-34 to construct the full-scale petrol plant. Capable of lifting 164 tons, here it lifts the last converter into position on No. 2 Stall. 'Stalls' were the six hydrogenation units where coal paste or creosote were made into petrol. Titan also lifted the converters for maintenance, and in 1994 served in dismantling Oil Works upon its closure.

GENERAL VIEW, OIL WORKS, 1935. In the distance is Newport Bridge, built by Dorman Long and Co. and opened in 1934 by HRH The Duke of York (later HM George VI). Crossing the Tees just upstream of Billingham Beck, it was the first vertical lifting bridge in England, and despite its 2,500 tons could be raised rapidly.

THE OIL JETTY, 1935. The first cargo of creosote for making petrol arrives for unloading from *Meryl* in January. The piling had been laid during the previous July. Middlesbrough ironworks' chimneys protrude in the background.

THE OIL JETTY, 1935. The first consignment of petrol is being loaded into *Otterhound* in April. In 1935 petrol was mainly despatched in tankers of 1,000 tons capacity.

OIL WORKS SITE, 1935, as seen from the Middlesbrough bank of the Tees. The riverside petrol storage tanks and jetty can be seen.

Above: LOADING PETROL. Ex-army tankers are taking on Oil Works petrol after the Second World War. During the war ICI made aviation fuel, including iso-octane fuel for RAF fighter planes in pursuit of flying bombs. After the war, ICI sold its own Imperial brand from petrol stations, and also sold on to other companies. These tanker lorries are labelled Shell Mex BP Ltd and National Benzol Mixture. It was said that traffic fumes on North East roads had an odour all their own!

Right: 'ROLL OUT THE BARREL' or, more strictly, drums with reinforcement bands for rolling. Petrol production ended at Billingham in 1956, but the new Wilton plant piped petrol under the Tees to Oil Works which continued to store, blend and distribute until closure in 1994 after fifty-nine years. From 1951 the high pressure converters produced carbonylation alcohols for plasticisers.

Above: ICI BILLINGHAM WHARVES. ICI had other wharves along the Tees at Billingham Reach. Here, a steam-sail ship is moored.

Left: LOADING FERTILIZER. Bagged ammonium sulphate is being loaded at an ICI wharf, pre-1958. North African phosphate rock for fertilizer manufacture was also unloaded here.

FIRELESS STEAM LOCO. Raw materials and goods were also transported by rail. There were up to eighty miles of line on the ICI site. Wherever flammable vapours might be present, *Fireless*, charged from a steam main, could operate.

HAVERTON HILL SOUTH. Engine no. 65830 passes Haverton Hill South signal box with a load.

Left: ON-SITE TRANSPORT. Saddle-tank engine no. 38 hauls trucks between two silos. No. 5 silo is on the right.

Below: ICI SIDINGS. This photograph gives some idea of the vast scale of operations. Metal wagons are mainly in evidence, but some wooden ones are still in use. By the mid-1930s there were ten miles of surfaced roads and some seventy miles of standard-gauge track inside the seven-mile perimeter fence, increasing after the war to around eighty miles, with twenty locomotives and over a thousand rail wagons.

Seven

ICI People at Work and at Leisure

ICI FROM THE AIR in the late 1960s near its maximumum extent, when around 19,000 were employed on the Billingham site. (Norman McCord)

WEST GATE. Workers pour out from West Gate into Chilton's Lane. There is a box for medical certificates on the left. Great queues of road traffic built up in the mornings at Billingham Bottoms as staff and workforce came in from far and wide. Many local people came in on foot or on bicycle.

LEAVING WORK, early 1950s. The nitro-chalk tower looms over the West Gate. A bus station was later built to the left, and buses then exited into Belasis Avenue. There were six gates in the main factory fence: West, East, North, Acrylics, CCF and Newport. Paddy's Crossing led into South Site.

Right: BILLINGHAM OLD STATION. Many employees travelled by train. The level crossing bottleneck on Station Road was by-passed during the Second World War by a dual carriageway and overbridge to the west, parallel with Billingham Beck.

Below: A GATE NEAR ENGINEERING AND APPRENTICE TRAINING, early 1960s.

ENGINEERING TRAINING. Apprentice training schools for trade skills were an important aspect of entry to work.

SECRETARIAL TRAINING. Girls were introduced to secretarial work. There are shorthand symbols on the blackboard and a typewriter keyboard chart is on display. Appropriately, perhaps, the typewriters are by Imperial!

Right: FOOD. Feeding the multitude was also important. Two women prepare food in a canteen bakery.

Below: THERE WERE a number of canteens, cafeterias and restaurants on site.

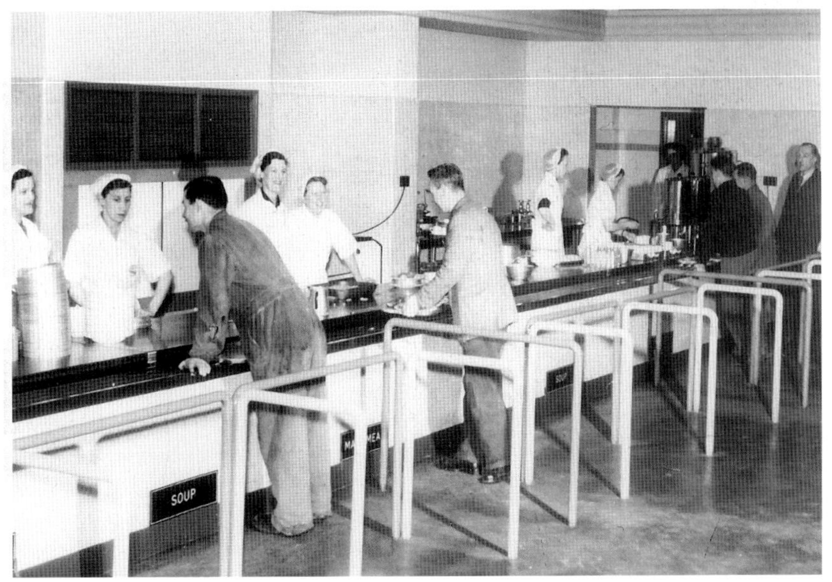

FIRE PRACTICE AT ELMWOOD HOUSE, 1941. A stirrup pump is being demonstrated. During the war camouflage paint, a smoke screen and decoy sites were among the precautions taken, but only nuisance raids occurred. The Synthonia Theatre in Belasis Avenue was hit and left 'open at both ends'. The RAF were billeted in Billingham, and German POW camps were sited at Cowpen and Wolviston.

AT WAR. Women were recruited as ICI workmates. Jean Watson recalls that schools were closed on outbreak and children taught in groups in houses. Later, there was a British Restaurant behind Billingham South School providing workmen's lunches, and teachers got meals from it. A barrage balloon and a gun were sited at Central Avenue corners, and smoke screens arose from big drums with wicks. Women used spare wicks as curling pins! Tank traps were sited in St John's church field; the ditches became ponds with tadpoles in!

SEWING ON LABELS.

WORKMEN POSE ON A SADDLE TANK ENGINE.

LONG SERVICE AWARD. A nurse receives a wrist watch.

LONG SERVICE AWARD DINNER, 1966. ICI's practice was to give awards for 20, 30, 35 and 40 years service. At the front is the host for this table, Gordon Winn (Technical Dept Manager) and Mrs Winn. From the left are clockwise Mr and Mrs Fred Snowdon, Mr and Mrs Jim Holdsworth, Mr and Mrs Ken and Vera Chapman.

NEW MAIN OFFICES, 1964. These opened in late 1959 in Belasis Avenue and complemented Chilton House. Four people on the right give scale to this massive block designed by ICI Billingham Division Architects' Dept with W.B. Edwards & Partners and Ove Arup and Partners. The grand entrance hall, where art exhibitions were held, the paternoster lift and the views from the roof were notable. (Vera Chapman)

PATENTS DEPARTMENT, c. 1980. By this date the above building was ICI Agricultural Division's Main Offices. Graham Rushton and Ken Chapman are seen here on the occasion of a visit of Japanese patent attorneys from Yuasa and Hara, Tokyo, to discuss the patenting in Japan of the car exhaust catalyst honeycomb invented by ICI chemists at Billingham. This was then an offshoot of the main thrust of Billingham's research and development, but it has since become central.

HRH THE PRINCE OF WALES' VISIT, 1930. Also in the picture is Sir Harry McGowan KBE (ICI Chairman 1930-1950). ICI Synthetic Ammonia and Nitrates Ltd was later to become ICI Fertilizers and Synthetic Products Ltd.

RAMSAY MACDONALD'S VISIT, October 1935. Seen on the left, he is officially opening the Oil Works hydrogenation plant. He had been the Prime Minister until earlier that year. With him are Sir Harry McGowan (see above) and Kenneth Gordon (Plant Manager). By 1935 ICI had a staff of 900 and a workforce of around 10,000.

HM KING GEORGE VI AND QUEEN ELIZABETH'S VISIT, 1941.

HRH THE PRINCE PHILIP, THE DUKE OF EDINBURGH'S VISIT, 1960s.

OIL WORKS SAFETY SHIELD, 1980. Tom Hay, Works Engineer of Oil Works, presents the Safety Shield to Bag Store Workshops Maintenance Group. Bag Store? Names associated with former uses of buildings tended to stick despite changes in function! Safety was a vital consideration throughout the chemical industry.

OIL WORKS TROPHY, 1984. Tom Hay presents the Safety Shield in the third quarter of 1984 to the Inst/Electrical Section.

BOWLING SECTION, SYNTHONIA CLUB, 1930. Dr E. Slade plays the first wood on the new green. Taking part in sport and leisure activities and in the life of the town was encouraged by ICI. The name 'Synthonia' is, of course, derived from 'Synthetic Ammonia' in the firm's original name.

OPENING OF THE CRICKET FIELD, 1930.

OIL DIVISION TEAM, 1930.

ANOTHER CRICKET GROUP.

RUGBY 1st XV, 1930.

FOOTBALL TEAM, 1931. Nitrates Group staff team.

SPORTS DAY SCENE.

PIONEER BOARD PLANT SPORTS, 1936-37. Back row, left to right: C. Lovery, J. Nicholson, R. Pearson, J. Williamson, P. Corey, T. Forster, R. Kinghorn, -?-, A. Woodhouse, M. Robinson, H. Rowntree, H. Nichol, J. Kinghorn, W. Kidd, -?-, W. Peacock, D. Old, C. Watson, J. Street, -?-. Front row: -?-, -?-, I. Maddren, Carr, T. Blyth, Taggert, Patterson, B. Spears, A. Chamberlain, F. Caswell, Wilks, S. Cresswell and H. Harper.

'PIONEER' PORTLAND CEMENT TEAM, 1935-36. Part of Casebourne Works, the inter-departmental final was against South South (Cassel Works). The result was 3-3. Kick-off was at 3.00pm and the game finished at 5.45pm.

SYNTHONIA CLUB BILLIARDS, 1930. Thompson played with W. Smith in the afternoon.

Left: SYNTHONIA CLUB DOG SHOW.

Below: SYNTHONIA PLAYERS, c. 1950.

Opposite above: SYNTHONIA PLAYERS, probably a post-production party. Dr Fleck is in the centre, seated.

Opposite below: NORTON HALL SMOKER, c. 1950s. At Norton Hall staff club are, left, Mr Healey and, centre, Dr Fleck. Alexander Fleck (1889-1968) trained as a lab boy at Glasgow University and followed an academic career there. From 1917 he was chief chemist to Castner Kellner Alkali Co. at Wallsend and became Works Manager. At Billingham from 1927, he had wider scope in planning and operating the new works, becoming Chairman of Billingham Division in 1937. From 1944 he was an ICI Director, mainly responsible for Billingham and for developing the Wilton site. As ICI Chairman from 1953 to 1960 he was 'the wise father of a very large family'. He became a Baron in 1961.

Acknowledgements

My thanks are gratefully given to those who have allowed me to copy their photographs, given their time for discussion and helped in my search. I have been careful to establish ownership and ensure permission to reproduce in this book. I apologize for any omissions or errors. Actual photographers, where known, are named beside their photographs.

Substantial numbers of photographs are by courtesy of ICI. The Forum, Billingham, the schools of Billingham, the Green Dragon Museum, Stockton-on Tees, Tom Hay and Les Jobson have also contributed generously from their collections.

Other contributors and helpers are ABC Heating Ltd, G. Barber, Ken Bates, Ken Bradley, Norman Brookes, David Campbell, John Casey, Kenneth H. Chapman, Eddie Curran, Michael Cuthbert, Darlington Branch Library, Doreen Davies, Addie Dick, Ailsa Dick, Rosemond Dry, Frank and Millie Elstob, Susan Godson, Gordon L. Hollis, Darren Holmes, Shirley Ince, Ethel Jobson, John LeRoy, Anne Liddle, Mrs Lightowler, Rachael Mason, G.A. Maxwell, Pauline McMaster, Mrs McTimoney, Norman McCord, Jean Orridge, Mr Patterson, F.W. Perfitt, Julian Phillips, J. Pollitt, Sister Emelda Paul, Margaret Rees, Mark Rowland-Jones, Tony Simpson, Kathleen Smith, Mrs A. Southeran, Maureen Stead, Winifred Still, Arthur Stimpson, Revd Father David Taylor, Michael Tennant, David M. Tomlin, Mrs Wallace, Jean Watson and David Wells.

Permissions to include photographs have been given by the *Evening Gazette*, Teesside, the *Hartlepool Mail*, Turners Photography, the University of Newcastle upon Tyne and The Francis Frith Collection, Shaftesbury, Dorset, SP7 8AT.

Francis Gerard Owen's book *Billingham from earliest times to the modern day* has provided substantial background information. I have also drawn upon a number of ICI publications.